Verbal Reasoning Tests Explained

Verbal reasoning tests are often a mystery to parents and their children. Why are they used? What kind of questions do they contain? How can my child prepare for a verbal reasoning selection test? This book will help you to understand verbal reasoning tests and ensure that your child is familiar with the questions they contain.

Athey Educational

Athey Educational
Tibthorpe
East Yorkshire
YO25 9LA

© **Athey Educational 1996**

ISBN 1 871993 10 5

Why do Grammar schools use verbal reasoning tests as part of their selection process?

A child's verbal reasoning ability is a good indicator of future academic success. It is not surprising, therefore, that Grammar schools invariably use verbal reasoning tests as part of their selection process.

These tests usually contains a hundred questions to be completed in fifty minutes. This inevitably places considerable pressure on children as the average time available to complete each question is only thirty seconds.

Some questions are not too difficult for many children but are included to assess how quickly children can process verbal information. Other questions are more difficult and assess whether children can solve problems. So, the ability to solve problems and work quickly are both important in completing a test successfully.

How will practice help my child?

Practice on verbal reasoning tests will not increase your child's verbal ability but will provide experience of the types of question included and the experience of working at the speed necessary to complete the paper. This in turn will increase your child's confidence and ensure that he performs at his best.

How should I use this book?

Verbal reasoning tests contain a variety of question types which have been shown to measure some aspect of verbal ability. Forty types of question are included in this book. Each question type is explained with reference to a typical set of questions from one of the test papers in the Secondary Selection Portfolio. Detailed advice is given on the best way to solve each question type by working through one or more of the examples. Additional questions are often included so that you can work these through with your child using the method described.

The verbal reasoning papers in the Secondary Selection Portfolio have been designed to help parents identify areas of difficulty. Ideally, you should work through the examples in this book before your child attempts a verbal reasoning practice paper. However, if your child continues to experience difficulty with a particular question type work through the examples again and discuss the various strategies suggested for solving that question type. Where a number of strategies are suggested let your child decide which one he prefers. He may well have a greater understanding and feel more comfortable with a strategy he has selected. As your child becomes more familiar with the question types it may not be necessary to follow the suggested approaches so meticulously, and short cuts may become apparent for solving some questions.

Do encourage your child to make notes on the answer paper. This can be very helpful as rough working is often essential to answer a question quickly and correctly.

As your child progresses through the practice papers and gains confidence in recognising question types he may be tempted to ignore the instructions. This should be discouraged as variations in instructions are quite common and often place a different slant on the question.

What is computer marking?

Grammar school selection tests are increasingly being designed to facilitate computer marking. A separate answer sheet is provided and the child is instructed to place a mark in a box to indicate which possible answer they have selected. It is simply a different way of recording an answer and does not affect the skills required to answer the question.

Type 1 (From Paper 1)

Each of the following sentences has two words which should change places with each other in order to make sense. Underline BOTH of the words in each case.

1. *The <u>quietly</u> moved <u>burglar</u> through the house.*

2. *Before Paul went to <u>teeth</u> he cleaned his <u>bed</u>.*

3. *Can this jump over you wall?*

4. *It an is offence to stop your car on a motorway.*

8. *Please door you close the will.*

★ ★ ★ ★ ★ ★ ★ ★ ★ ★ ★ ★ ★ ★ ★

Initially, the child should try to ignore the word-order and concentrate on what the sentence really means. Often the solution is then quite straightforward. If difficulty is encountered the following strategies can be used.

Either, (a) to look for phrases which stand sensibly by themselves, or (b) to look for phrases where the word order seems correct, but the meaning is nonsensical.

For example, in Question 1, 'through the house' has a sensible word order. It seems likely, therefore, that the words which need to change places are elsewhere in the sentence. Thus, we have narrowed the search down to the first part of the sentence, ie 'The quietly moved burglar'. This phrase does not make sense and the child will need to consider what new word order is necessary to make the phrase sensible. The child should now encounter little difficulty in deciding that 'The burglar moved quietly' is the only reasonable sequence. Thus, the words 'burglar' and 'quietly' are the words which need to change places.

If we look at Question 2 we can see that, again, the sentence can be divided into two parts: 'Before Paul went to teeth' and 'he cleaned his bed'. In this case the word order in both sections sounds familiar. The second phrase in particular does make sense. In the first phrase the problematic word is 'teeth', but where was Paul going? The only place Paul could be going is 'bed'. It seems fairly clear, then, that to make the meaning of the sentence sensible we would have to exchange one word from each part. It does not need much reflection to realise that the two parts should be 'Before Paul went to bed' and 'he cleaned his teeth'. The two words are therefore 'bed' and 'teeth'.

Type 2 (From Papers 1 & 2)

A B C D E F G H I J K L M N O P Q R S T U V W X Y Z

Examples from Paper 1.

The alphabet above can be used to help you with some of the following questions. In each question write in the brackets the missing numbers or the missing letters.

9. *A , Z , B , Y , (**C**) , (**X**) , D , W .*

10. *S , Q , O , M , (**K**) , (**I**) .*

12. *A , O , B , N , C , M , D , (_ _ _) , (_ _ _)*

14. *J , A , B , K , C , D , L , E , (**F**) , (**M**) .*

★ ★ ★ ★ ★ ★ ★ ★ ★ ★ ★ ★ ★ ★ ★

The best strategy when attempting to answer questions of this type is to look for the pattern which is always present in letter sequences. It is wise to use the alphabet provided by drawing loops from one letter to another or by drawing loops between the letters in the the question. It is then much easier to see any pattern which is contained within the series of letters.

When there is a series of single letters, such as the examples above from Paper 1, it is useful to see first of all if the pattern is one which involves adjacent letters or alternate letters. Question 9 is an example of an alternate letter pattern. Starting from the first letter, every alternate letter is jumped and the pattern is A, B, C, D. The other alternate pattern in this question starts from the second letter. The pattern in this case is one which goes backwards, ie Z, Y, X, W.

The adjacent pattern of letters exemplified in Question 10 is just as straightforward. The child needs to refer to the alphabet and to draw loops over the letters (as on the alphabet above) in the same order as those in the question. This will bring out the pattern which in this case is every second letter starting from S. The pattern is thus S, Q, O, M, K, I.

Question 14 combines two sequences, ie A, B, C, D, E, F and J, K, L, M.

The alphabet above is to help you work out the rule which connects each pair in the following rows. There is a different connection for each row. Write the next pair in the brackets provided.

20. AC $\overbrace{}^{BC}$, DF $\overbrace{}^{EF}$, GI $\overbrace{}^{HI}$, JL $\overbrace{}^{KL}$, MO ^{NO}, **(PR)**

59. AD , BE , **(CF)** , DG , **(EH)** , FI , GJ

⋆ ⋆ ⋆ ⋆ ⋆ ⋆ ⋆ ⋆ ⋆ ⋆ ⋆ ⋆ ⋆ ⋆ ⋆ ⋆ ⋆

When there are pairs of letters in the series it is often sensible to deal with the first letter of each pair in order to find a pattern. If we consider Question 59 there does not appear to be an obvious pattern in the series. However if we look at the first letter of each pair, the pattern becomes quite clear, ie A , B , ⋆ , D , ⋆ , F , G. The missing letters are 'C' and 'E'. So far, the following stage has been reached:

AD , BE , **(C_)** , DG , **(E_)** , FI , GJ .

Turning to the other letter of each pair, the sequence is as follows: D , E , ⋆ , G , ⋆ , I , J. In this example the pattern is the same as that for the first letter of each pair and the missing letters are 'F' and 'H'. Hence, the complete sequence is:

AD , BE , **(CF)** , DG , **(EH)** , FI , GJ .

The letter patterns in some questions may not be as simple as the example above. However, they should not be too difficult to discover using a variation of this strategy. Question 20, for example, follows the pattern above, but two letters are omitted between each of the first letters and each of the second letters in the series. The sequence of the first letters of each pair is as follows: A , D , G , J , M , ⋆ . If loops are drawn between these letters on the alphabet provided, the pattern will become clear. The missing letter is obviously 'P'. Before moving on to the final letter of each pair this letter should be written in the brackets. The second letters of the pairs can be worked out in exactly the same manner. Questions 58 and 60 (Paper 2) are similar, but each uses a pattern of alternate letters in the alphabet for the first and second letter of each pair.

Type 3 (From Papers 1 & 2)

Example from Paper 1.

15. *Joan and Mary enjoy playing hockey. Karen and Joan enjoy netball. Karen and Mary enjoy swimming. Which girl enjoys both swimming and hockey?*

(Mary)

J	M	K
h	ⓗ	
n		n
	ⓢ	s

Examples from Paper 2.

A, B, C, D, E and F are six boys. A, D and E go to Park School whilst the others go to Mill End School. B, C and E wear school caps. C, D and F wear grey shirts. Now answer the following questions.

A	B	C	D	E	F
P	M	M	P	P	M
	c	c		c	
		g	g		g

4. *Which boy who wears a grey shirt goes to Park School?*   **(D)**

5. *Which boy who attends Mill End School does not wear a school cap?*   **(F)**

⋆ ⋆ ⋆ ⋆ ⋆ ⋆ ⋆ ⋆ ⋆ ⋆ ⋆ ⋆ ⋆ ⋆ ⋆ ⋆

It is very difficult for many children to attempt to retain several items of information in their heads while at the same time re-ordering this information. When questions require this strategy it is an easy matter to jot down a simple grid at the side of the page containing all the necessary information to solve the problem. To do so only takes a few seconds yet it saves so much time compared with mentally going over and over the information given.

It is only necessary to use single letters to indicate the separate pieces of information. Thus, in Question 15 from Paper 1, which is a simple example of this type, the column headings would simply be the initial letters of the girls' names and the information under the headings would be the first letter of the various pastimes. If we look at the grid drawn next to Question 15 we can clearly see that Mary is the only girl who enjoys both swimming and hockey.

This approach is even more advantageous when there are a series of questions connected with the given information. Questions 4 to 7 from Paper 2 afford a good example of this. If the grid next to these questions is examined it can be seen that 'P' and 'M' stand for Park School and Mill School respectively, whilst 'c' and 'g' represent the wearing of caps and grey shirts. The questions can now be answered easily. For example, Question 4 asks 'Which boy who wears a grey shirt goes to Park School?'. Three columns contain a 'g' (grey shirt). On reading up each of the columns it can be seen that only one column also contains a 'P' (ie wears a grey shirt and also attends Park School). This boy is 'D'.

Type 4 (From Papers 1 & 2)

Examples from Paper 1.

16. *In a kitchen cupboard there are three pots containing different items. The rice is on the right of the flour and the sugar is on the right of the rice. Which item is in the middle?* **(Rice)**

17. *Tom has more marbles than Wendy. Wendy has more marbles than Debbie but less than Emma and John. Who has less marbles than the others?* **(Debbie)**

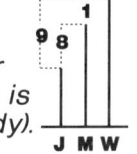

＊ ＊ ＊ ＊ ＊ ＊ ＊ ＊ ＊ ＊ ＊ ＊ ＊ ＊ ＊

For these questions the child should always write the information given, either in a shorthand form or as a quick diagram. For example, in Question 16 the child need only write 'F' for flour, 'R' for rice and 'S' for sugar. The first thing to write down at the side of the page is the first item of data, ie 'the rice is on the right of the flour'.   F   R   (ie the 'R' on the right of the 'F').

The next stage is for the child to write down the final piece of information, ie 'the sugar is on the right of the rice'.   F   R   S   (ie the 'S' on the right of the 'R'). The answer to the question is 'Rice' as the rice is in the middle.

With questions that refer to size or quantities, the best procedure is for the child to draw lines relative to the sizes or quantities given in the question. If we look at the diagram related to Question 17 you will see that the line labelled 'T' has been drawn longer than the line labelled 'W' because Tom has more marbles than Wendy. Likewise the line labelled 'D' is shorter than 'W'. The lines 'E' and 'J' are longer than 'W' but no information is given to tell us if these should be longer than 'T'. This is irrelevant because the question asks 'Which child has less marbles than the others?' As Debbie has the shortest line she has the least marbles.

Example from Paper 2.

36. *Mark is eight centimetres taller than John who is nine centimetres shorter than Wendy. So, (Mark is seventeen centimetres taller than Wendy, Wendy is one centimetre taller than John, Mark is one centimetre shorter than Wendy).*

＊ ＊ ＊ ＊ ＊ ＊ ＊ ＊ ＊ ＊ ＊ ＊ ＊ ＊ ＊

As in the previous example, Question 36 should be tackled by drawing lines to represent the three children. The line drawn to represent Mark should be taller than John's line with a figure 8 written in the space between the tops of the two lines to stand for the difference between the two heights. Wendy's line should be taller than both John's and Mark's with a figure 9 written between the top of Wendy's line and John's line. It can now be seen that the only true statement from those given is the one which states that Mark is one centimetre shorter than Wendy.

Type 5 (From Paper 1)

In each sentence below underline TWO words, one from each set of brackets, which complete the sentence in the best way.

18. *Finger is to (<u>hand</u>, thumb, nail) as Toe is to (shoe, heel, <u>foot</u>).*

21. *Sun is to (day, brother, hot) as Moon is to (white, man, night).*

＊ ＊ ＊ ＊ ＊ ＊ ＊ ＊ ＊ ＊ ＊ ＊ ＊ ＊ ＊

The best way to solve this question type is to quickly read the first word in conjunction with the three words in the first bracket looking for a connection between each of them and the first word. For example, referring to Question 18, finger - hand (a finger is one of the projections at the end of a hand), finger - thumb (a thumb can be found next to one of the fingers), finger - nail (a nail can be found on a finger).

The next step is to follow this procedure for the second word in conjunction with the three words in the second bracket. Thus, toe - shoe (toes are protected by a shoe), toe - heel (toes and heel are at opposite ends of a foot), toe - foot (a toe is one of the projections at the end of a foot).

We can clearly see that the two words which should be underlined are 'hand' and 'foot' because they have the same connection with 'finger' and 'toe'. Of course, the child does not have time to jot down the connections as we have done, they must be remembered. In practice this is not easy and it is usually necessary to check back to the first part of the question and then perhaps to the second part again to confirm that the right connection has been made.

The following questions require exactly the same procedure as Type 5, although the question format is different.

4

Type 5a (From Paper 2)

In each of the following questions there should be two pairs of words which have the same connection between them. The second word of the last pair has been left out. Find this missing word by looking for the connection and write it in the brackets. All the correct answers have FOUR letters.

73. GLOVE , HAND ; SHOE , (＿＿＿＿)

74. BLOW , TRUMPET ; BEAT , (＿＿＿＿)

Type 5b (From Paper 2)

In the following questions each star stands for a letter.

94. ARM is to E**** as L** is to KNEE.

95. TRUNK is to T*** as S*** is to FLOWER.

Type 6 (From Paper 1)

In each of the lines below, ONE of the words from each group will go together to make another proper word. Remember that the word from the first group always starts the new word. Underline the TWO words.

26. <u>over</u> / across / through   cat / purr / <u>lap</u>

28. by / to / <u>in</u>   rain / storm / <u>hale</u>

★ ★ ★ ★ ★ ★ ★ ★ ★ ★ ★ ★ ★ ★ ★

If the answer is not seen very quickly a logical approach to solving this type of question ought to be adopted. This entails considering each of the three words in the first group in turn and mentally coupling them with each of the words in the second group. As soon as a proper single word is encountered the child need go no further.

If we use Question 26 as an example of this approach, the child will need to start with the first word of the first group, ie 'over'. This is then successively linked with each of the words of the second group, producing: 'overcat', 'overpurr' and 'overlap'. The word 'overlap' is a real word and the words 'over' and 'lap' should be underlined.

It may be necessary to try far more couplings than in the example above. If we consider Question 28, for instance, the child would need to try all possible couplings before finding a proper word.

'byrain' , 'bystorm' , 'byhale'   'torain' , 'tostorm' , 'tohale'   'inrain' , 'instorm' , **'inhale'**

Type 7 (From Paper 2)

Each of the following rows has a different rule connecting the numbers. Find the rule and write the next number in the brackets.

1. $6 \overset{+9}{,} 15 \overset{+9}{,} 24 \overset{+9}{,} 33 \overset{+9}{,}$ (**42**) .

2. $84 \overset{-1}{,} 83 \overset{-2}{,} 81 \overset{-3}{,} 78 \overset{-4}{,}$ (**74**) .

3. $110 \overset{-13}{,} 97 \overset{-13}{,} 84 \overset{-13}{,} 71 \overset{-13}{,}$ (**58**) .

★ ★ ★ ★ ★ ★ ★ ★ ★ ★ ★ ★ ★ ★ ★

To find the missing number or numbers in a series the child must discover the pattern which the series follows. The best way to do this is to decide which of the four operations, ie addition, subtraction, multiplication or division, connects the first two numbers in the series. If the second number is higher than the first, the appropriate operation will be either addition or multiplication. If the second number is lower than the first, the operation will be either subtraction or division. The child should write in the spaces above and between the adjacent pairs of numbers the connection between them.

In Question 1 the second number is larger than the first number so the appropriate operation is either addition or multiplication. The difference between the numbers is 9 and this is written between the numbers. However, we need more information before we can decide how the series progresses. If we now look at the difference between the next two pairs we can see that the difference is also 9. The pattern is one of increasing by 9 each time and the missing number is therefore 42. In Question 2 the sequence is a decreasing one. However the numerical gap between each pair is not the same; it increases by one each time. To follow the pattern the missing number must be 4 less than 78, ie 74. The third question also has a decreasing pattern but this time it is a uniform pattern, each gap is 13. The missing number is thus 58.

33. If mushrooms are a kind of plant and all plants are not animals, which of the following must then be true? Underline ONE sentence only.

    (a) Mushrooms are related to toadstools.

    (b) Mushrooms are good to eat.

    (c) <u>Mushrooms are not animals</u>.

    (d) Mushrooms are animals because they are not green.

★ ★ ★ ★ ★ ★ ★ ★ ★ ★ ★ ★ ★ ★ ★

With this type of question the child needs to concentrate solely on the information given in the question and to totally disregard any other related information that she may know to be true.

The information provided in the question is (a) mushrooms are plants, and (b) plants are not animals. This information and NOTHING ELSE should be used to find the answer. Thus, although mushrooms may be related to toadstools, or mushrooms may be good to eat, these are not the required answers because the question asks 'which of the following must THEN be true', ie which statement logically follows from the given information. The only statement which logically follows from the information given in the question is 'Mushrooms are not animals'.

Type 9 (From Papers 1 & 3)

Examples from Paper 1.

A B C D E F G H I J K L M N O P Q R S T U V W X Y Z

The alphabet above is provided to help you find the answers to the following code questions. Your answers need to be written in the brackets.

34. If $\overset{+1\ +1\ +1\ +1}{O\ N\ R\ S}$ means POST , then GDKL means **(HELM)**.

35. If URKP means SPIN , then JCV means (_ _ _ _ _). **count 2 back**

36. If 6554 means $\overset{6554}{FEED}$, then 257 means (_ _ _ _ _).

37. If OFAB means RIDE , then CFOB means (_ _ _ _ _). **count 3 back**

★ ★ ★ ★ ★ ★ ★ ★ ★ ★ ★ ★ ★ ★ ★

In this type of question there is a connection between each code letter and its corresponding letter in the proper word. In Question 34 the 'real' letters are the ones which immediately follow the 'code' letters in the alphabet. With the exception of Question 36, where the code is the number which corresponds to the position of the letters in the alphabet, the 'real' letters can be found by either counting backwards or forwards from the 'code' letters.

Example from Paper 3.

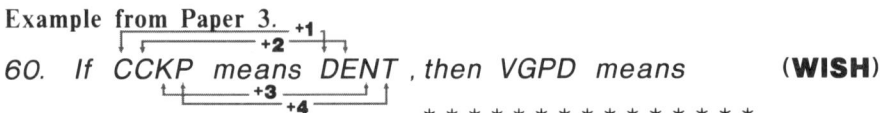

60. If CCKP means DENT , then VGPD means **(WISH)**

★ ★ ★ ★ ★ ★ ★ ★ ★ ★ ★ ★ ★

In Question 60, the connection between the code letters and their corresponding real letters does not follow a uniform pattern. The pattern is progressive. The first letter of the real word is the letter following the code letter, ie D replaces C. However, the second letter is two letters in the alphabet after the corresponding code letter, ie E replaces C. The third letter is three letters after the code letter and the fourth letter is four letters after the code letter. So, V stands for W (W = V + 1); G stands for I (I = G + 2); P stands for S (S = P + 3); and D stands for H (H = D + 4).

Type 10 (From Paper 1)

In each of the following sentences there is a FOUR letter word hidden. The hidden word can be found by looking at words in the sentence next to each other. Find the hidden word and write it in the brackets.

42. They ha<u>ve st</u>olen our money. **(VEST)**

43. We shall order coffee. (_ _ _ _ _)

★ ★ ★ ★ ★ ★ ★ ★ ★ ★ ★ ★ ★ ★ ★

The best way for a child to find the answers to this variety of question is to look at each of the words in the sentence or phrase in conjunction with its neighbouring word. We start by focussing on the last three letters of the first word because we know that at least one letter must be found in the adjoining word and the hidden word contains four letters.

If we refer to Question 42, the last three letters of the first word are 'hey'. The first letter of the second word is 'h'. Thus the first four-letter word is 'heyh'. This is not a real word so we must move on to the next two sets of four letters. These are 'eyha' and 'yhav'. As neither of these letter combinations is a proper word we now combine the end of the second word with the beginning of the third word. In this case we have ; 'aves', 'vest', and 'esto'. A proper word hidden between two adjacent words has been discovered so the child need proceed no further; the correct answer is 'vest'.

This type of question is not difficult to understand or answer correctly, but the successful child is the one who can answer these questions rapidly. Practice will increase your child's speed.

Type 11 (From Paper 1)

In each of following questions you must underline TWO words, one from each group, which have the SAME or almost the same meaning.

49. TRAP , LAUGH , <u>STARTLE</u> : FALL , HIT , <u>SHOCK</u>

50. MESSY , DIRTY , BLOT : ROOM , UNTIDY , SCRIBBLE

51. CELEBRATION , CHEERS , BIRTHDAY : MEETING , OPERA , FESTIVITY

* * * * * * * * * * * * * *

The best strategy a child can adopt when looking for similar or opposite meanings in questions such as those above, is to compare each of the first three words one at a time with each of the words in the second group.

For example, in Question 49 the child needs to compare the word 'TRAP' from the first group with 'FALL', 'HIT', and 'SHOCK' from the second group in order to find a word with a similar meaning. If, as in this case, a word with a similar meaning cannot be found, the child must then compare the second of the first three words with each of the members of the second group. Thus, 'LAUGH' should now be compared with 'FALL', 'HIT', and 'SHOCK'. Again, no similar meaning can be found. The child should now finally compare the last of the first three words with 'FALL', 'HIT', and 'SHOCK'. Here it can be seen that 'STARTLE' has a similar meaning to 'SHOCK' and also that this is the only pair with a similar meaning.

It is most important with this question type that the child reads the instructions carefully to establish whether she needs to find words with similar or opposite meanings.

Type 12 (From Paper 1)

In the following questions there should be three words in each group. The missing word goes with its partners in the same way as the middle word in the first group of three words goes with its partners. Write the missing word in the brackets.

57. $\overset{1\ 2\ 3\ 4}{SOUP}$ $\overset{1\ 2\ BC}{(SOIL)}$ $\overset{ABCD}{PILE}$ $\overset{1\ 2}{COWS}$ $(\textbf{CORN})$ $\overset{B\ C}{URNS}$

60. $\overset{1234}{PAIL}$ $\overset{1\ B4\ D}{(POLE)}$ $\overset{A\ B\ C\ D}{DONE}$ $\overset{1\ 4}{HOLD}$ $(\textbf{HIDE})$ $\overset{B\ D}{FIVE}$

63. $\overset{1\ 2\ 3\ 4\ 5\ 6}{BASKET}$ $\overset{DA26}{(GOAT)}$ $\overset{A\ BCDEF}{ORIGIN}$ $\overset{2\quad 6}{PRAISE}$ $(\textbf{SURE})$ $\overset{A\quad D}{UNISON}$

64. SHORE (ROB) MAYBE   STAFF (_ _ _ _) SPITE

* * * * * * * * * * * * * * *

This type of question is often confusing for children because of the large amount of information which has to be carried in their heads during the process of working out the answer. If any difficulty is encountered the following is a reasonably foolproof approach. It involves writing numbers or letters above the first three words of each question. The strategy outlined below may take a little time but it ensures that the answers will be correct.

The procedure is as follows (refer to worked examples above):

(a) The child should write a number over each of the letters of the word in front of the brackets.

(b) Consecutive letters of the alphabet should be written above the word which comes after the brackets.

(c) Finally, either letters or numbers are written above the letters of the word in the brackets. If, for example, the first letter of the word in brackets has come from the word which has been numbered then the appropriate number is written above this letter.

(d) To work out the unknown word in the second set of brackets the child simply has to repeat the above process from a to c, using the two new words and the same relationship discovered in the first group.

In each of the questions below, ONE letter must be removed from the first word and placed either at the beginning or end of the second word, or in the middle. This will then leave two new words which are BOTH real and properly spelt. All of the other letters must be left in the same order. Write BOTH new words in the brackets.

70.   DEAR and RINK become (_ _ _ _ _) and (_ _ _ _ _)

71.   GROW and ALE become (_ _ _ _ _) and (_ _ _ _ _)

72.   PIT and SOON become (_ _ _ _ _) and (_ _ _ _ _)

73.   MEN and IN become (_ _ _ _ _) and (_ _ _ _ _)

★ ★ ★ ★ ★ ★ ★ ★ ★ ★ ★ ★ ★ ★ ★

If the child has any difficulty answering this type of question a good approach is to concentrate initially on the first word of the given pair and find out which letter can be removed from it to leave a proper word.

In Question 72 the first word to consider is 'PIT'. If each of the letters is removed in turn it is easy to see when a proper word is left. The possibilities are as follows:

★**IT** , P★T , PI★

The only letter which can be removed to leave another real word is the letter 'P'; in this case the word 'IT' is left. The next stage is to discover where the letter 'P' can be placed into the second word. This can be accomplished in much the same way as the first stage; the child should mentally place the relevant letter in each of the possible places one at a time until a proper word results. So, the following combinations are possible:

PSOON , **SPOON** , SOPON , SOOPN , SOONP

The only proper word is SPOON.

This approach can be adopted in all questions of this type. It should not be necessary to jot anything down on the paper since the child can easily carry out the above operations in her head.

Each of the following questions has three pairs of words. The third pair go together in the same way as the first two pairs. Complete the last pair of words by writing the missing word in the brackets.

76.   ~~b~~one - one ; ~~p~~ink - ink ; ~~s~~our - (**OUR**)

77.   s~~l~~ew - sew ; t~~r~~ip - tip ; f~~l~~an - (**FAN**)

    1234 **4321**   **1234** **4321**   **1234**

78.   evil - live ; deer - reed ; plug - (**GULP**)

79.   peach - ace ; smelt - elm ; croak - (_ _ _ _)

80.   f~~u~~sed - fed ; b~~ra~~in - bin ; a~~do~~pt - (_ _ _ _)

81.   ballot - boat ; signal - sail ; tamper - (_ _ _ _)

★ ★ ★ ★ ★ ★ ★ ★ ★ ★ ★ ★ ★ ★ ★

This type of question is a much simpler version of Type 12 questions; it requires exactly the same kind of manipulation but this time only the letters from one word instead of two are involved in making the required word.

The best way for the child to tackle this kind of question is to number the letters of the first word of each pair, either mentally or by actually writing above it, and then to find out which numbered letters are used to make up the letters of the second word.

As an example let us refer to Question 81. The first thing to do is to number the letters of the word 'ballot' and then find out which numbered letters make up the word 'boat'.

               1 2345 6 **1 5 26**   **1234 56** **1 5 26**   **1 2 3 4 5 6**

81.   b a l l o t - b o a t ; s i g n a l - s a i l ; t a m p e r - (tear)

You can see from the above that the letters of 'boat' are the 1st, 5th 2nd and 6th letters of 'ballot'. Similarly, 'sail' is also made from the 1st, 5th, 2nd and 6th letters of 'signal'. It follows that the missing word will be the 1st, 5th, 2nd and 6th letters of 'tamper', ie 'tear'.

It is not necessary to follow the above procedure meticulously for each question of this type; many of the relationships between the first and second words are plain to see without adopting this approach. Questions 76 and 77, for example, should be quickly obvious.

5412 2463 5163

The words LOAD, DONE, LANE are coded 2463, 5412, and 5163, but not necessarily in that order. Write down the codes for the following:

6423
82. *NODE* **(6423)**

5162
83. *LAND* **(5162)**

* * * * * * * * * * * * * * * *

Initially many children have difficulty with this type of code question. However, there should be no problem once the child has been reassured that there are always a number of clues which can be used to solve them. For example, in the questions above there are several clues which can be used:

(i) Two words begin with the letter 'L' whilst the remaining one begins with 'D'. This means that the child need only look for two initial numbers which are the same and then concentrate on the third set of code numbers which begins with a different number (ie 2463) since these must stand for 'DONE'. These numbers should be written above the word 'DONE' and then written above the letters D, O, N, and E in the other two words. The remaining number codes can then be worked out with little difficulty.

(ii) Alternatively, the child might look at the letters which end the three words. In this case two of the three words end in 'E'. So, the code for 'LOAD' must be '5412' because the other two code words end in '3'.

(iii) Another clue can be found by focussing on the second letter of each word. Two of the three words have an 'O' as the second letter. The word which has a different second letter must, therefore, be represented by the number set which has a different second number. Thus, 'LANE' must be represented by 5163.

Note that it is necessary for the child to use only one of the suggested clues in order to work out the word codes. The only reason more than one clue has been cited is to demonstrate that there are usually several alternative ways of arriving at the solution. Finally, once the corresponding numbers and letters have been discovered it is now a straightforward procedure for the child to provide the codes for 'NODE' and 'LAND' because all the numbers for these letters have been found. The answers to Questions 84 - 86 (Paper 1) can be worked out in a similar way, ie initial letters, final letters and inner letters can all be used for the solutions. However, for Questions 87 - 89 (Paper 1) neither initial letters nor final letters can be used because all are different. With a little thought, however, the child should be able to see several more ways to solve the code. For example, 'HERS' starts with 'H'and 'GASH' ends with 'H', or 'RAGE' and 'GASH' both have the letter 'A' as their second letter. Similarly, the letters 'S', 'G', 'R' and 'E' appear in two of the three words and can be used to break the code.

Type 16 (From Paper 1)

For the following questions you will need to write in the brackets ONE letter which ends the first word in each pair and begins the second word. The SAME letter must be used in BOTH sets of brackets.

90.	CRAC	( )	NOW	RIS	( )	NEEL
91.	DOZE	( )	URSE	BEGI	( )	OSE
92.	TOUC	( )	ALT	RUS	( )	ALF
93.	PEA	**(T)**	AME	SEN	**(T)**	IGHT

* * * * * * * * * * * * * * * *

The most common mistake children make with this type of question is to forget that the SAME letter must be included in each set of brackets.

The best strategy is for the child to think of a letter which will end and begin the two incomplete words on either side of the first brackets. Once this has been done the child should then see if the SAME letter will now fit into the other set of brackets.

If we use Question 93 as an example, the child might decide that 'L' will fit satisfactorily into the first brackets in order to make the words 'PEAL' and 'LAME'. However, this will not do as an answer since when 'L' is fitted into the second brackets of that question it makes the words 'SENL' and 'LIGHT'. As 'SENL' is not a real word, 'L' is obviously not the correct letter. The child should then look for another letter which fits into both brackets. The only letter which fits satisfactorily into both is the letter 'T'. It makes the words 'PEAT' and 'TAME' on one side and 'SENT' and 'TIGHT' on the other.

Type 17 (From Paper 1)

The following are types of simple crosswords. Only one word has been included in each case. Each of the other words to be included can be found on the left of the puzzle. Complete each puzzle by fitting these five words in the correct positions. The first puzzle has been completed to show you.

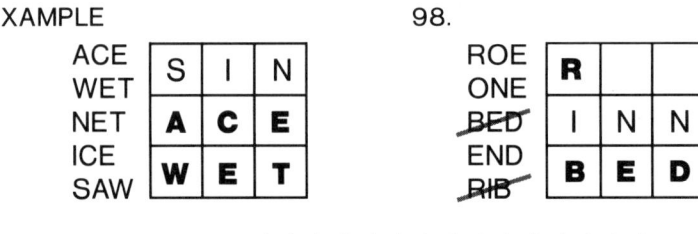

EXAMPLE

ACE
WET
NET
ICE
SAW

S	I	N
A	C	E
W	E	T

98.

ROE
ONE
~~BED~~
END
~~RIB~~

R		
I	N	N
B	E	D

★ ★ ★ ★ ★ ★ ★ ★ ★ ★ ★ ★ ★ ★ ★ ★

The easiest method of approaching these simple crossword problems is for the child to look for words which fit in the crossword in only one position. In Question 98 the word given to start the child off is 'INN'. In this word the letter 'I' can only serve as the middle letter of the word 'RIB' (no other word has the middle letter 'I'). Once this word has been included in the crossword the child can then carry on in the same way; the only word with an initial letter of 'B' is 'BED', and so on.

In Question 99 (Paper 1), the only word which begins with 'E' is 'ELK'. Similarly, in Question 100 the only word with 'A' as its middle letter is 'MAD' and the only one with 'W' at its centre is 'EWE'.

Type 18 (From Paper 2)

Each of the following sentences has one word with its letters jumbled up. Unjumble the letters and write the proper word in the brackets.

8.   L I O N I V is a stringed instrument.   **(VIOLIN)**

9.   B E G A C A B is a green vegetable.   (_ _ _ _ _)

10   G O T C A T E is a kind of small house.   (_ _ _ _ _)

★ ★ ★ ★ ★ ★ ★ ★ ★ ★ ★ ★ ★ ★ ★ ★

Children can often decipher a word with its letters in the wrong order quite easily. However, if the real word is not perceived immediately then it is a good idea for the component letters to be written down at the side of the paper in a random order. The arrangement can either be in the form of a circle or simply a random grouping (See above). When this has been done, combinations of letters present in the proper word can often be seen more easily.

In addition, the written clues concerned with the identity of the real word should be used to concentrate the mind on words belonging to that particular family. Thus, in Question 8, the child only needs to think of the names of all the stringed instruments before alighting on the answer. With Question 9, for example, a mental scanning of all the different kinds of green vegetable should suffice.

Type 19 (From Paper 2)

In each of the following questions there are TWO words in the brackets which are connected with the words in capital letters. Underline these two words.

15.   ALSATIAN SPANIEL   (kennel , bone , <u>labrador</u> , collar , <u>pekinese</u>)

16.   SHEET BLANKET   (sleep , chair , pillow , mattress , wardrobe)

17.   STREET LANE   (road , pedestrian , cars , avenue , junction)

★ ★ ★ ★ ★ ★ ★ ★ ★ ★ ★ ★ ★ ★ ★ ★

In this question type there are four words (including the two words in capitals) that belong to the same 'family'. The best strategy for a child to adopt is to think of a possible connection between the two words in capital letters and then to see if two of the words inside the brackets have the same connection.

If we refer to Question 15, the words written in capitals are both names of breeds of dog and, although there may be words contained in the brackets which are closely connected with dogs, the child should only be looking for the names of breeds of dog amongst the words inside the brackets. Similarly, in Question 16 the child should be looking inside the brackets for the names of items which are usually placed on a bed, and not for words simply connected with the bedroom.

Type 19a (From Paper 5)

There is a connection between the words in the groups below. The words in each group have a different connection from words in each of the other groups. The groups are labelled A to E.

A	B	C	D	E
College	Tanker	House	Lamb	Tiny
School	Cruiser	Cottage	Kitten	Microscopic
Academy	Tug	Bungalow	Calf	Small

Each of the following words has a connection with only ONE of the above groups. Write the correct group letter in the brackets next to each word. For example, 'Speedboat' is (B) because a Tanker, a Cruiser and a Tug are all types of boat. A speedboat is similar to these and not to any of the other groups of words.

9.   Mansion **(C)**   10.   Little **(E)**

11.   Gosling ( )   12.   Liner ( )

★ ★ ★ ★ ★ ★ ★ ★ ★ ★ ★ ★ ★ ★ ★ ★

Although the format of the questions above is from Type 19 questions they require similar thought processes, ie grouping words into families. The child needs to decide the family to which each of the words belong. Thus, MANSION is a type of dwelling so it belongs to (C). LITTLE is a word describing smallness so it fits into category (E), and so on.

Type 20 (From Paper 2)

The following table shows the average rainfall in centimetres at five different places during the months from April to August 1995.

	APRIL	MAY	JUNE	JULY	AUGUST
Adcaster	13.8	14.3	17.8	20.4	24.9
Barchester	10.9	13.2	17.1	20.9	24.2
Colsterworth	17.1	18.3	19.9	23.7	26.8
Dorking	13.2	14.6	19.3	22.2	24.4
Emster	14.6	16.8	19.1	24.8	24.6

Now answer the following questions by underlining the right answers in the brackets.

38.   *In which month did Emster have less rain than Adcaster?*

(April , May , June , July , <u>August</u>)

39.   *In which month was Dorking wetter than Emster?*

(April , May , June , July , August)

43.   *Which place had the same rainfall in May as Dorking had in April?*

(Adcaster, Barchester, Colsterworth, Emster)

★ ★ ★ ★ ★ ★ ★ ★ ★ ★ ★ ★ ★ ★ ★ ★

To answer this type of question satisfactorily a child must know and understand how information is displayed in tabular form. Each reading or figure in the table has two dimensions. For example, if we refer to the figure at the top of the first column, ie 13.8, this is the amount of rainfall, in centimetres, which fell on Adcaster during the month of April. One dimension is at the end of the horizontal line on which the figure appears and the other dimension is vertically above it.

If we look at Question 38, the child needs to compare two places in order to find out the month during which one place had less rainfall than the other. In this case the child must compare the two horizontal lines of information which refer to the two villages mentioned. Thus, the information which the child should compare is as follows:

	APRIL	MAY	JUNE	JULY	AUGUST
Adcaster	13.8	14.3	17.8	20.4	24.9
Emster	14.6	16.8	19.1	24.8	24.6

It can easily be seen that there is only one month where the rainfall is less in Emster, ie August. All the other questions which require information to be used from tables should be approached by the child in the same manner.

For the following questions pretend that all the words have been written BACKWARDS and then put in alphabetical order. Which word would come . . .

		2	**4**	**3**	**1**	
66.	*FIRST?*	(*imitate,*	*potentate,*	*orientate,*	*facilitate*)	

		2	**5**	**1**	**4**	**3**
67.	*LAST?*	(*station,*	<u>*attention,*</u>	*ration,*	*function,*	*traction*)

68.	*SECOND?*	(*picture,*	*fracture,*	*stricture,*	*epicure,*	*nature*)

* * * * * * * * * * * * * * *

Whenever a child encounters a question which involves sorting words into alphabetical order the same strategy should always be adopted whether the words are to be ordered as written or as if they were written backwards.

When ordering the words as written, the first thing to do is to focus on the first letter of each word. If the task is to order the words as if they were written backwards the focus is the last letter of each word. Let us look at Question 66. In this question there are four words, imitate, potentate, orientate and faciltate.

As the child is asked to say which of the words would come first if they were written backwards, the last letter of each word should be looked at first. In the above example the last letter of each word is identical so we must move to the next letter. Here too, the letters are the same. If we gradually move inwards, one letter at a time, it can be seen that this is also the case for the next two sets of letters. We now come to the letters which are the fifth from the end of each of the words. Here we have two words with 'i' and two words with 'n' as the letters fifth from the end. As the letter 'i' comes before 'n' in the alphabet then one of the two words with 'i' in this position must come first, ie imitate or facilitate.

We have to move in by one further letter to decide which of these two words it should be. The relevant letters are 'm' and 'l'. The answer is 'facilitate' since 'l' comes before 'm' in the alphabet.

Each of the following questions has words written in code. Underline the correct answer in the brackets. There is a different code in each question.

2 5 3 4 7 9 8   **R E S T**
86. *If 2534798 means MONSTER then 8947 means* (*stem, must, <u>rest</u>, most, rent*)

3 6 9 8 2 1
87. *If 369821 means FORGET then 861 means* (*rot, got, get, rug, for*)

* * * * * * * * * * * * * * *

Once the child is familiar with a straightforward method of solving this question type, these questions will be relatively easy to tackle successfully.

The best strategy is for the child to either write the code numbers over the real word in the correct place, or to write the letters of the real word over the code numbers. If we use Question 86 as an example this should be easier to follow:

2 5 3 4 7 9 8
2534798 means MONSTER. Write the numbers over the letters like this - M O N S T E R

This shows that 2 = M, 5 = O, 3 = N, 4 = S, 7 = T, 9 = E and 8 = R. It is now easier to work out what 8947 means - 8 = R, 9 = E, 4 = S, 7 = T, - the word is REST. All such questions should be approached in exactly the same way.

Six months ago Deborah started to collect foreign coins. She bought five every month. Now answer the following questions.

99. *How many has she bought already?*   **(30)**

100. *How many will she have collected six months from now*
     if she continued to collect at the same rate?   (_ _ _)

* * * * * * * * * * * * * * *

Type 23 questions involve pure mathematical operations and are a familiar aspect of mathematical activities which take place at school. Referring to Question 99, if Deborah bought five coins every month for a period of six months, then she bought 30 coins in total, ie 6 x 5. It is equally obvious that a further 30 will be purchased during the coming six months, thus making a total of 60 coins bought altogether.

Type 23a (From Paper 4)

The questions below are all concerned with numbers. For each question work out the answer and write the number in the brackets.

62. *8 is smaller than this number by 15.*   (_ _ _ _)

63. *If we add seven and then another 8 the answer is 23.*   (_ _ _ _)

64. *If we multiply it by 6 the answer is seventy-two.*   (_ _ _ _)

* * * * * * * * * * * * * * *

The questions above are concerned with mathematical word puzzles and need to be approached in a systematic way. Sometimes there is only one step required to reach the answer, as in Question 62. Thus, if 8 is 15 less than the number we are looking for then we arrive at this number by adding 8 and 15. The answer is therefore 23.

Similarly, in Question 64 only one step is required. If the number we are looking for multiplied by 6 is 72, then we arrive at this number by dividing 72 by 6. The answer is 12.

Question 63 requires two steps. In this question three numbers added together give the answer 23. We are given two of the numbers and the third number is the one we are looking for. If we subtract the two known numbers from 23 the remaining number is the one we are looking for. So, 23 take away 7 is 16, and 16 take away 8 is 8. 8 is therefore the number we are looking for.

Type 24 (From Paper 3)

In each of the following sentences there is one word with some letters missing. Each of these words has THREE letters missed out. Without changing the order of these missing letters you can make another word. Write this other word in the brackets.

7. *The dog scched because it had fleas.*   (**RAT**)

8. *The ctaker looks after the school building.*   (_ _ _ _)

* * * * * * * * * * * * * * *

The best strategy to adopt when tackling this type of question is first of all to use the words which surround the incomplete word in order to guess what the sentence should say. Each of the sentences has been constructed so that this is always possible.

Using Question 7 as an example, it is reasonably clear that the incomplete word is 'scratched' because scratching is a common activity for dogs afflicted with fleas. Once the child has discovered the identity of the incomplete word this should be written in full over the word with the letters missing. Each of the letters of the incomplete word should now be crossed off the complete word in order to see which letters remain (See above for an example).

Type 25 (From Paper 4)

In the following questions only ONE of the words in the brackets can be made using the letters of the word in capitals. Underline this word.

69. *SCRUPULOUS (sculls , flour , scour , spruce , unless)*

70. *CANDIDATURE (duration , dream , dread , antler , crest)*

* * * * * * * * * * * * * * *

The best way to approach these questions is to focus on each word in the brackets in turn, in order to compare each of its component letters with each of the letters of the word in capitals. This can be done either mentally or by physically marking the letters when they are matched with a letter from the word written in capitals.

Let us look at Question 70. The first word in the brackets is 'duration'. The first six letters can all be found in the word 'CANDIDATURE' but there is no 'O'. The next word is 'dream'. All of these letters can be found with the exception of the final letter 'M'. The next word is 'dread'. All of these letters can be found in 'CANDIDATURE', including both 'D's so this is the word we are seeking.

The child should be encouraged to re-check that the correct word has been chosen. Mistakes can easily be made, particularly as all the words can almost be completed with the available letters. Errors can occur when the same letter is used twice in a word, eg 'sculls' in Question 69. Two 'L's are required but there is only one in 'SCRUPULOUS'.

The alternative version of this type of question requires the child to underline the only word which CANNOT be made from the appropriate word in capitals.

Type 26 (From Paper 4)

A B C D E F G H I J K L M N O P Q R S T U V W X Y Z

86. How many letters of the alphabet between H and U are NOT in the
word DISPENSATION? (_ _ _)

87. Which three letters of the word REPRESENTATION
are consecutive letters of the alphabet? (_ _ _) and (_ _ _) and (_ _ _)

⋆ ⋆ ⋆ ⋆ ⋆ ⋆ ⋆ ⋆ ⋆ ⋆ ⋆ ⋆ ⋆ ⋆ ⋆ ⋆ ⋆

This type of question requires no explanation or strategy since the child is expected simply to read the question and to act on its instructions. The only useful advice which can be given here is for the child to read the question slowly so that the instructions and meaning are absolutely clear and to re-read it several times until its contents are absolutely understood.

Type 27 (From Paper 4)

Underline the word in the brackets which makes the best sense in the following sentences.

89. Doctors prescribe medicine because it is (unpalatable, incurable, hospitalised, beneficial, odorous).

90. John had hurt his leg and was (embodied, excluded, prevented, distanced, adjusted) from the football team.

⋆ ⋆ ⋆ ⋆ ⋆ ⋆ ⋆ ⋆ ⋆ ⋆ ⋆ ⋆ ⋆ ⋆ ⋆ ⋆ ⋆

To successfully complete this type of question the child needs a good vocabulary. The correct answer is arrived at by mentally fitting each of the words in the brackets into the sentence to find out which one makes the most sense.

Referring to Question 89, the following sentences are mentally constructed:

1) Doctors prescribe medicine because it is unpalatable.

2) Doctors prescribe medicine because it is incurable.

3) Doctors prescribe medicine because it is hospitalised.

4) **Doctors prescribe medicine because it is beneficial.**

5) Doctors prescribe medicine because it is odorous.

From the above possible constructions the fourth sentence is the only one which is suitable since doctors do not prescribe medicine because it is unpalatable, incurable, hospitalised, or odorous.

When working out the answers to the this type of question it is not necessary for the child to write anything; the construction can be carried out quickly and efficiently in the head.

Type 27a (From Paper 7)

In the following you will need to underline ONE word from each set of brackets in order to make the sentence into one that makes the most sense.

91. The (gardener, teacher, doctor) wrote on the (pad, soil, blackboard) with a piece of (glass, cheese, chalk).

92. (Six, Three, Five) added to (two, four, ten) equals (eleven, twelve, nine).

⋆ ⋆ ⋆ ⋆ ⋆ ⋆ ⋆ ⋆ ⋆ ⋆ ⋆ ⋆ ⋆ ⋆ ⋆ ⋆ ⋆

These questions closely resemble those of Type 27. However, the procedure is somewhat different.

The best strategy for the child to adopt is to initially concentrate on the end of the sentence. In Question 91 the latter part of the sentence reads 'wrote on the (?) with a piece of (?)'. Since the only sensible item that can be used for writing which is contained within the last set of brackets is 'chalk', the appropriate word in the second bracket is obviously 'blackboard'. The child can now move mentally to the first bracket and deduce that the correct word to underline here is 'teacher'. The sentence now reads 'The *teacher* wrote on the *blackboard* with a piece of *chalk*.'

Similarly, the child should go to the last part of Question 92 in order to work out the right answer. The last bracket contains three numbers, (eleven, twelve, nine). The child should focus on each one of these in turn and see if any two of the numbers, one from each of the first two brackets, together add up to the appropriate answer. There are no pairs which total either eleven or twelve. However, five and four together add up to nine. Thus, the correct answer is '*Five* added to *four* equals *nine*.'

Examples from Paper 6 (90 to 97) should be approached in exactly the same way as those illustrated below from Paper 7, once the child has worked out the code as explained for Type 15 questions.

Examples from Paper 7.

Each of the letters in the word STIMULATE has a different number value: S = 1 , I = 2 , M = 3 , U = 4 , L = 5 , A = 6 , T = 8 and E = 10. Now work out the answers to the following questions and write the answers as a NUMBER.

84. $\overset{2}{I} \times \overset{4}{U} + \overset{1}{S}$ **(9)**

85. $\overset{3}{M} + \overset{10}{E} - \overset{5}{L}$ **(8)**

86. $L \times A - T$ (_ _ _)

87. $I + L + M$ (_ _ _)

★ ★ ★ ★ ★ ★ ★ ★ ★ ★ ★ ★ ★ ★ ★

This type of question should not be difficult for children to answer. However, care should be taken when substituting the letters for numbers. To be absolutely certain of correct substitutions the child should cross out the letters in the questions and write the appropriate numbers over the top. Once the substitutions have been made, the various arithmetical operations should be tackled in the order they occur in the question. Question 84, (I x U + S = ?), after substitution becomes (2 x 4 + 1). The operations should be attempted in the same order as that given in the question. Thus, the first operation is (2 x 4). The answer to this first part of the question is 8, and this is then coupled with the last part. This second and last section is, therefore, (8 + 1). Clearly the correct answer is 9.

Questions 85 and 86 should be tackled in the same way. Question 85 asks (M + E - L = ?). After substitution this becomes (3 + 10 - 5 = ?). The first operation is (3 + 10). The answer is 13, and this leads to the second operation, ie 13 - 5. The answer is, therefore, 8.

With this type of question the child should be particularly vigilant with regard to the last section of the instructions. In the question above the child is asked to give the answer as a NUMBER. Sometimes the child is asked to give the answer as a LETTER. This means that an extra step is involved, ie a re-substitution of the numerical answer back to the letter it represents.

Type 28a   (From Paper 15)

The words COST, TRIP, OVER are coded 5719, 7830 and 9024, but not necessarily in that order. Write down the codes for the following.

6.   *PROVE*   (_ _ _ _ _ _)

7.   *CREEP*   (_ _ _ _ _ _)

8.   *IS IT SEPTIC?*   (_ _ _ - _ _ _ - _ _ _ _ _ _?)

Use the above coded letters and write the answers to these sums as letters. Each answer is a three-letter word.

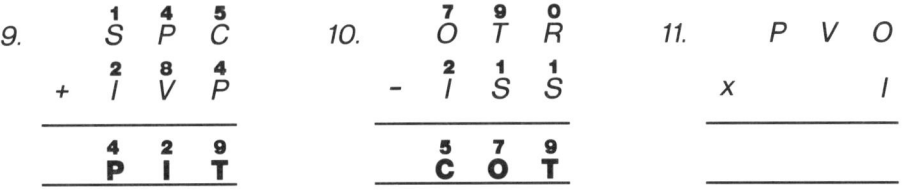

Questions 6 to 8 above are examples of Type 15 questions. Since the method for solving these has already been explained we will assume that the child has obtained the correct answers and will be able to substitute numbers for the letters in questions 9 to 11.

The answer to the sum in Question 9 is 429. The last stage is to convert the numbers back to letters. If a proper word is not obtained the child will know the answer is wrong and should work the sum again. In the example above the answer 429 is converted to PIT. This is a properly spelt word so the child will be reasonably certain that this is the correct answer.

In Question 10 the numerical answer is 579. This is now converted back to letters and the word COT is formed.

In the example below each word has had ONE letter changed to make it into a new word. FELT has been made into FEET by changing the L to E and FEET has been made into MEET by changing the F to M. In the next groups of words the middle word is missing. Find this word using the rule explained above.

F	E	L	T		71.	M	I	N	T	72.	F	O	O	T
F	**E**	**E**	**T**			(	**I**		**T**	)		(**F**	**O**		)
M	E	E	T				F	I	S	T			F	O	A	L

* * * * * * * * * * * * * * * *

In Question 71, changing only one letter at a time, 'MINT' has to be changed into 'FIST' in two moves. The first thing to do is to see which letters in the first and the last word have not been changed. The second and fourth letters of both words remain the same, ie 'I' and 'T'. These can now be written in (See above).

We now know that either the first or the third letter of the first word was changed to make the middle word. We also know that the first move was either to change the 'M' in 'MINT' for 'F' or the 'N' in 'MINT' for 'S'. These are the only two possibilities because we know that the last word is 'FIST'. The middle word can either be 'FINT' or 'MIST'. The correct answer is 'MIST' because there is no such word as 'FINT'.

If we look at Question 72, the first two letters of the given words have remained the same, so to make the middle word either the second 'O' or the 'T' need to be changed first. Thus, either the 'O' is changed to 'A' or the 'T' is changed to 'L'. This would make either 'FOAT' or 'FOOL'. Clearly, the right answer is 'FOOL'.

The following map is a map of a small part of the east side of a certain country. The railway lines and the roads on which the people can travel between towns N , O , P , Q , R and S are shown. Answer the questions by writing the answers in the brackets.

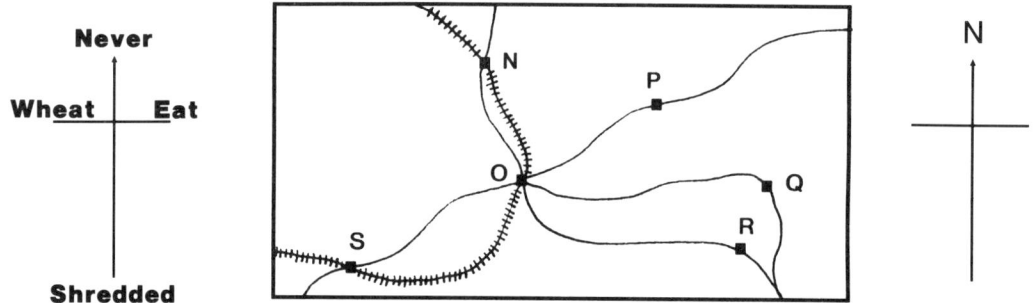

78. To travel from Q to P which town would you have to pass through? (_ _ _)

79. Which is the busiest town shown on the map? (_ _ _)

80. Which town is furthest south? (_ _ _)

81. Between which TWO towns do the railway and the road
closely follow the same route? (_ _ _) and (_ _ _)

82. Which TWO towns are south-west of one other town? (_ _ _) and (_ _ _)

* * * * * * * * * * * * * * * *

To answer this type of question the child will need to have attained simple map reading skills.

Questions 78, 79 and 81, for example, require knowledge of how roads and railways are represented on maps and an awareness that the busiest towns will have more lines of communication passing through them, ie transport routes.

Questions 80 and 82 require knowledge of compass points. The points, other than North, are not usually included in the compass drawn at the side of maps. Children may find it useful to learn a mnemonic as an aid to remembering the compass points in the right order. Starting from North, and moving in a clockwise direction, the main points can be recalled by reciting the words 'Never Eat Shredded Wheat'.

Type 31 (From Paper 6)

In the following sums there are several figures which have been missed out. Where there is a missing number you will see a box. Write the missing numbers in the boxes.

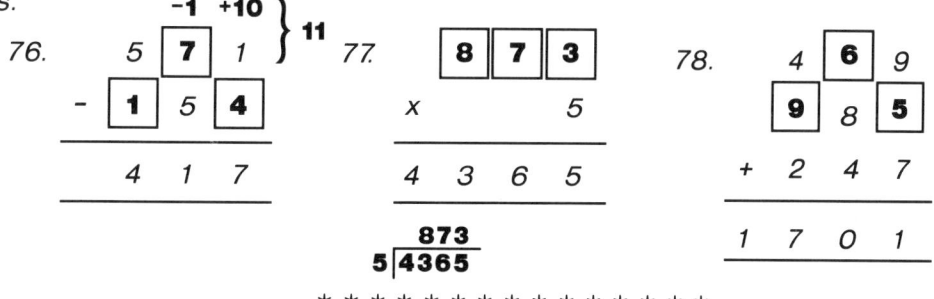

★ ★ ★ ★ ★ ★ ★ ★ ★ ★ ★ ★ ★ ★ ★ ★ ★

Children need to draw on their basic mathematic skills in order to successfully tackle this type of question.

Let us look at each of these questions in turn.

SUBTRACTION

In Question 76 we must first look at the units column and ask - 'What do we take away from 1 to leave 7?', ie 1 - ★ = 7 . This is a seemingly impossible question since no number can be subtracted from 1 to leave 7 as the answer. Clearly, the number at the top must be 11 and a ten from the adjacent column must have been taken to transform the 1 to 11. Thus, the number at the top of the tens column must be reduced by one in order to transform the original 1 in the units column to 11. The question now becomes 'What must we take from 11 to leave 7?'. The answer is 4 and this figure should be written into the answer.

We now move to the tens column, but having done so we must remember that the missing number at the top has had to be reduced by one to make the calculation in the units column possible. The next question to be asked is 'From what do we have to subtract 5 to leave 1?', ie ★ - 5 = 1. The answer is 6. However, we need to remind ourselves that this number has had to be reduced, so the original number must have been 7. This figure must now be written into the answer. The last step is simple, 5 - ★ = 4, so the right answer must be 1.

Now that the sum is complete it can be quickly checked to see if the answer to the sum is correct. If the sum is correct we know that the correct numbers have been written in the boxes.

Another way to tackle this question is to use the knowledge that the opposite of subtraction is addition. (For example, 4 + 7 = 11, so 11 - 4 must be 7 and 11 - 7 must be 4). So, instead of working the sum through as a subtraction sum to find the missing numbers your child may find it easier to work it through as an addition sum, ie adding 417 to ★5★ to arrive at the answer 5★1.

MULTIPLICATION

Just as the opposite of addition is subtraction, the opposite of multiplication is division. The same permanent connection holds for any three numbers using the operation of multiplication and division, eg 4 x 3 = 12 so 12 ÷ 4 must be 3.

If we refer to Question 77 it will be seen that we can use this information to find the answer to the problem. The opposite of multiplication is division so if the top number multiplied by 5 gives 4365, then 4365 divided by 5 must result in the top number. Thus, the answer is 873.

ADDITION

The child should approach Question 78 in the same logical way as the subtraction problem. The first column to deal with is the units column. The question to be posed is 'If I add 9 and 7, what must I add to the result to make the answer end in 1?'. 9 + 7 is 16 so the nearest number ending in 1 must be 21. This means that 5 must have been added to the 9 and 7 to result in 21. Thus, 5 should be written into the answer.

We now move to the tens column, remembering that as the total in the units column was 21 we need to 'carry' 2 tens into this column. In case we forget this, it is sensible to add it immediately to either of the known numbers in the tens column. The same procedure is followed and the question to be posed is 'If I add 8 and 4 and 2 (carried from the units column), what must I add to the result to make the answer end in 0?'. 8 + 4 + 2 is 14 so the nearest number ending in 0 must be 20. The number 6 must be added to 14 to give the answer 20. The number 6 should now be included in the answer.

The final step is identical, 4 + 2 + 2 (carried from the tens column) + ★ = 17. The answer is, therefore, 9.

Type 32 (From Paper 7)

In the following questions one word is different from the others in the list in some way. Underline the word in each line which is the 'odd one out'.

5. (hat , *window* , shoes , coat , socks)

6. (gas , oil , glass , coal , electricity)

٭ ٭ ٭ ٭ ٭ ٭ ٭ ٭ ٭ ٭ ٭ ٭ ٭ ٭ ٭ ٭

The best approach with 'odd one out' type of questions is to start with the first word in the list and to look for a connection with one of the other words in the brackets. If there is no connection, move to the second word in the list and repeat the process. In this way, if the child gradually moves along the list of words, a 'family of words' will begin to emerge. This will leave one 'outsider' which does not belong to the group.

Referring to Question 5, and starting with the first word 'hat', the child should attempt to form a connection with the second word, 'window'. There does not appear to be an obvious association, so step two is to try the first and third words: 'hat' and 'shoes'. In this case there is a possible connection. Both of these words refer to articles that are worn by people. This possible connection should now be checked by looking at the last two words in the list. As 'coat' and 'socks' are also items of clothing, the 'family of words' is that of 'clothing articles' and the 'odd one out' is obviously the word 'window'.

Type 33 (From Papers 7 & 10)

Example from Paper 7.

41. *If the following words were arranged in order of length with the longest first, underline the one which would be in the middle.*

    7 letters   **6 letters**   **5 letters**
    (*general* , neighbour , extend , definite , range)

Examples from Paper 10.

In each of the following questions you must underline the word which comes in the middle after the words have been arranged in order of sequence or size.

     5   2   4   3   1
15. (adult , baby , youth , *toddler* , embryo)

16. (eagle , sparrow , ostrich , wren , crow)

٭ ٭ ٭ ٭ ٭ ٭ ٭ ٭ ٭ ٭ ٭ ٭ ٭ ٭ ٭ ٭

Question 41 (from Paper 7) refers to the number of letters in each of the words and Questions 15 and 16 (from Paper 10) are concerned with word meanings. The child should write a number above each word according to its relative size or position in the sequence.

In Question 41 the first task is to find the shortest word, ie 'range'. The next two words are 'extend' with six letters and 'general' with seven. As there are five words in the list, the third word, 'extend' is the middle word.

In Question 15 the words could be ordered in sequence or size but the result is the same. The order is from youngest to oldest, ie embryo, baby, toddler, youth, adult. The middle word is 'toddler'.

Question 16 requires an ordering according to size. The smallest bird is a wren, then a sparrow, then a crow followed by an eagle and, largest of all, an ostrich.

Type 34 (From Paper 8)

60. *What relation is Mr Howe to his daughter's daughter?*

    (Father , Uncle , Nephew , *Grandfather* , Father-in-law)

61. *What relation is Mr White to his mother's sister?*

    (Uncle , Nephew , Niece , Brother-in-law , Cousin)

٭ ٭ ٭ ٭ ٭ ٭ ٭ ٭ ٭ ٭ ٭ ٭ ٭ ٭ ٭ ٭

These questions are all concerned with relationships within the family. The child needs to approach answering this question type in a logical, step by step, manner. Two steps are normally required Question 60, for example, asks the child to find the relationship between a person and his daughter's daughter. Step A is to find the relationship between the person and his daughter, ie 'father', and step B is to find the relationship between the father and the daughter of his daughter, ie 'grandfather'. Sketching a 'family tree' (see above) may be found helpful.

Type 35 (From Paper 9)

Red Black, Yellow and Green are four teams involved in a netball tournament. Each of the teams plays all the other teams once. There are six games in all. Reds beat Yellows but lose to Greens and Blacks. Blacks are only beaten by Greens. Greens beat Yellows. None of the games ended as a draw. Now answer the following questions.

70.   *How many games do the Reds win?*   (_ _ _)

71.   *How many games do the Blacks win?*   (_ _ _)

72.   *How many games do the Yellows win?*   (_ _ _)

72.   *How many games do the Greens win?*   (_ _ _)

★ ★ ★ ★ ★ ★ ★ ★ ★ ★ ★ ★ ★ ★ ★

For some questions that contain a lot of information the best strategy is to construct a simple grid. This was demonstrated for Type 3 questions. For the question above the best strategy is to write down all possible combinations in shorthand (See below). The result of each combination can then be entered using the information in the question. For example, the question tells us that 'Reds beat Yellow but lose to Green and Black'. This information provides the results for three matches. Using the rest of the information in the question we can complete the results for all six matches.

R plays B	R plays Y	R plays G	B plays Y	B plays G	Y plays G
B wins	R wins	G wins	B wins	G wins	G wins

Answering the questions is then straightforward.

Type 36 (From Paper 9)

In each of the following questions there are several numbers on the left hand side of the page. In each set of brackets write three of these numbers between the signs in order to make the number you are given.

91.   *4, 8, 10, 13, 25*   :   7 = (**25** - **10** - **8**)

92.   *3, 6, 8, 9, 10*   :   6 = (−   +   )

93.   *2, 4, 5, 20, 30*   :   3 = (÷   ÷   )

94.   *2, 4, 7, 9, 10*   :   18 = (x   ÷   )

★ ★ ★ ★ ★ ★ ★ ★ ★ ★ ★ ★ ★ ★ ★

These questions require a logical trial and error approach. For example, in Question 91 there are two subtraction operations required. In order to arrive at the answer 7, the numbers will probably start with the largest and progress to smaller ones. If the largest three are chosen the sequence will be 25 - 13 - 10. However, the answer to this is 2 and not 7. If the largest is missed out and the three next largest figures used, the sequence will be 13 - 10 - 8. This also cannot be the right combination because the answer would be negative. If we revert back to the largest figure and subtract the third largest and then the fourth largest, the sequence is 25 - 10 - 8. This is the correct sequence since the answer to this is 7. Question 93 can be tackled in the same way.

Another way to solve the above questions is to approach them in two parts. For example, if we look at Question 91 again, we know that the result of the second operation must be 7. If we try the first of the possible numbers from the list on the left, ie 4, and mentally place this in the last position, we know that in order to leave 7 the answer to the first operation must be 11.

[★ - ★]
7 = (★ - ★ - 4)   thus, 7 = (11 - 4)

We now need to look for a combination of two numbers which when subtracted give the answer 11. As there is no possible combination we know that 4 cannot occupy the last position in the brackets. The next possible number is 8. If 8 was the correct number in the last position in the brackets, the answer to the first operation would be 15 because -

[★ - ★]
7 = (★ - ★ - 8)   thus, 7 = (15 - 8)

Again, the next step is to find out if there is a combination of two numbers which will leave 15 after subtraction. Since 25 - 10 will make 15 we know that these three numbers must be the correct combination, ie 7 = (25 - 10 - 8). This method of starting with the highest number and mentally trying each of the possibilities in turn can be used with all the questions.

Type 36a (From Paper 17)

In each of the following questions select numbers from the left hand side of the page and write them in the brackets in order to make the number you are given. One of the numbers must be used TWICE.

33. 4, 9, 10, 13, 25   :   7 = (**25** - **9** - **9**)

34. 3, 4, 8, 9, 10   :   27 = (x   +   )

35. 2, 3, 5, 20, 30   :   7 = (÷   -   )

36. 2, 4, 7, 9, 16   :   60 = (x   -   )

★ ★ ★ ★ ★ ★ ★ ★ ★ ★ ★ ★ ★ ★ ★

These questions require a slight modification to the procedure used for Type 36 questions. For example, we know that one possible approach is to mentally place the first of the numbers on the left in the last position in the brackets and to continue from there. Thus, referring to Question 33, if we place 4 in the last position we know that in order to leave the answer 7 the answer to the first operation must be 11. However, as one of the numbers from the list on the left has to be used twice, either the 4 must be repeated or the two numbers in the first operation must be the same. Thus, so far we have either:

[11]   [11]
7 = (★ - 4 - 4)   or   7 = (★ - ★ - 4)

The second alternative cannot be correct because a number subtracted from itself leaves zero. Thus, if the last number in the brackets is 4 then this number must be repeated in the first operation. In which case the first number would have to be 15. Thus, 7 = (15 - 4 - 4). As 15 does not appear in the list this cannot be the answer. The next number to mentally place in the last position is 9. As before 9 would have to be repeated twice. We therefore have 7 = (★ - 9 - 9). If this part of the answer was correct the first number in the brackets would have to be 25. As 25 appears in the list this must be the correct answer.

Similarly, in Question 34 we place the first number on the left in the last position.

27 = (★ x ★ + 3)

If 3 is to be repeated, either one of the numbers in the first operation must be 3 or both of the first two numbers must be the same. If 3 is correct then the result of the operation must be 24.

[★ x ★]
27 = (24 + 3)

If 3 is the number which is not repeated then both of the first two numbers must be identical. This is clearly not the case because 24 is not a square number. This indicates that the answer would be as follows:

27 = (★ x 3 + 3)

If the above equation is correct the missing number would have to be 8. As 8 appears in the list, this must be the correct answer.

Type 37 (From Paper 10)

In the next lines write a number in the brackets which correctly completes the sum.

49.   54   -   29   =   5   x   (**5**)

50.   57   +   43   =   2   x   (_ _ _)

51.   8   x   5   =   87   -   (_ _ _)

54.   56   ÷   7   =   32   ÷   (**4**)

★ ★ ★ ★ ★ ★ ★ ★ ★ ★ ★ ★ ★ ★ ★

The equations above can be solved in a very straightforward manner. The child needs to find out the value on the left hand side of the equation and use this information to work out the missing number on the right hand side.

In Question 49 the value on the left hand side of the equation is 25, ie 54 - 29. This value is then mentally transferred to the right hand side. The child now needs to ask the question '25 = 5 x ?'. The answer is 5 and this is entered in the brackets as the answer.

Question 54 has the operation '56 ÷ 7' on the left hand side. The answer to this is 8. This is also the answer to the operation on the right hand side. The child should now answer the question '8 = 32 ÷ ?'. The answer is clearly 4.

Example from Paper 10.

88. *My watch is 6 minutes fast and the train which should have arrived at my station at 11.30 am is 5 minutes late. What time is it by my watch when the train arrives?*

(11-41 am)

Examples from Paper 12.

If the kitchen clock was five minutes slower than Peter's watch when Peter's watch stopped, answer the following questions.

32. *If Peter's watch stopped at 5.20 pm what time was it by the kitchen clock ten minutes later?*　　　　　　(_ _ _ _)

33. *What time was it by Peter's watch when the kitchen clock chimed 5.00 pm?*

(_ _ _ _)

★ ★ ★ ★ ★ ★ ★ ★ ★ ★ ★ ★ ★ ★ ★

Questions involved with time usually contain reference to either two watches, a watch and a clock, or a watch and train or bus which is early or late. Such questions are basically the same since one of the time pieces usually shows the wrong time and the child needs to transfer the time shown on one of the watches or clocks to the other. If the question involves a bus or train which is late and a watch which is wrong then both sets of information must be married together. In other words, if the train was 10 minutes late and the watch was 5 minutes fast then the person wearing the watch would have to wait 15 minutes for the train to arrive. Alternatively, if the train was five minutes late and the watch was five minutes slow, the train and the person would arrive at the station at the same time.

Let us look at Question 88. The train should have arrived at 11.30 am and it is five minutes late. Thus, it will arrive at 11.35 am. If we now consider the watch to find out what time it would be showing at this later time, it would be showing a time of six minutes ahead of 11.35 am because it is six minutes fast. Thus, the watch would indicate a time of 11.41 am.

Let us now turn to Questions 32 and 33. When Peter's watch stopped at 5.20 pm the kitchen clock would have shown a time of 5.15 pm because it was 5 minutes slower. Question 32 asks what time the kitchen clock would show ten minutes after the watch stopped. The answer, therefore, is 5.25 pm since this is ten minutes after 5.15 pm. Question 33 asks what time it was by Peter's watch when the kitchen clock chimed 5.00 pm. Since the kitchen clock was five minutes slower than the watch, the watch would have shown a time of 5.05 pm.

The following map shows the position of a school and the homes of five children, Andy (A), Betty (B), Carol (C), David (D) and Edward (E). Numbers refer to distances in metres.

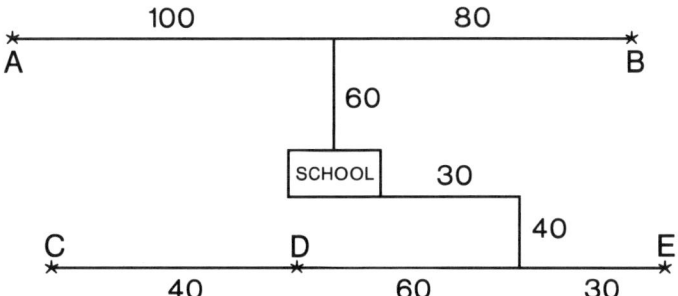

93. *How far does Carol walk to school?*　　　　　　**(170m)**

94. *Who walks further to school, Betty or Edward?*　　　(_ _ _ _ _ _)

95. *If Edward walks to school at a speed of 1 Km in ten minutes how long does the journey take him?*　　(_ _ _ _min)

97. *One morning David called for Carol and they walked to school together. How far did David walk that morning?*　　(_ _ _ _m)

100. *Who walks further to school, Andy or David?*　　(_ _ _ _ _ _)

★ ★ ★ ★ ★ ★ ★ ★ ★ ★ ★ ★ ★ ★ ★

Type 39 questions refer to maps or scale drawings. With regard to the questions above, the child should bear in mind that the various journeys referred to in the questions should be considered in stages. Thus, with regard to Question 93, the distance which Carol has to walk to school needs to be considered in a number of stages. First of all, Carol has to travel 40 m to get to David's house, then another 60 m to get to the intersection of the road which ultimately leads to the school, another 40 m and then another 30 m before actually arriving at school. The total journey is, therefore, 170 m.

If we now consider Question 94, Betty's journey has two sections to be considered whilst Edward's journey has three sections. Despite Edward having more sections, however, Betty's journey is the longer of the two because 80 m + 60 m is greater than 30 m + 40 m + 30 m.

Question 95 is concerned with speeds. In order to answer such questions the child must approach them in a logical fashion. Thus, referring to Question 95, if Edward takes ten minutes to walk a distance of 1000 metres (ie 1 Km), he would take one tenth of this time to walk one tenth of the distance. He would, therefore take one minute to walk a distance of 100 metres.

Type 40 (From Paper 18)

At the start of the season the members of Heaton United Football Team decided to try to score more than thirty goals and have less than fifteen scored against them in their first fifteen games. Graph 1 shows how many goals were scored against them in each of these fifteen games. Graph 2 shows how many goals they scored in these games. Each of the matches is labelled M1, M2, M3 up to M15.

GRAPH 1. GOALS SCORED AGAINST HEATON UNITED

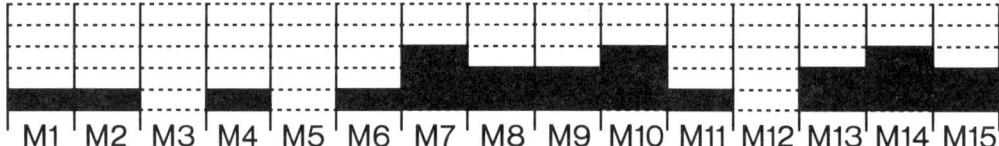

GRAPH 2. GOALS SCORED FOR HEATON UNITED

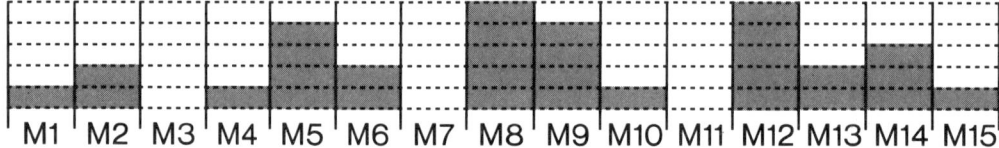

81.	Circle how many matches were drawn?	(0 , 1 , 2 , 3 , 4 ⑤ , 6)
82.	How many matches did they win?	(0 , 1 , 2 , 3 , 4 , 5 , 6)
83.	How many games did they lose?	(0 , 1 , 2 , 3 , 4 , 5 , 6)
84.	Did they score a total of more than 30 goals?	(Yes / No)
85.	Were less than 15 goals scored against them?	(Yes / No)

⋆ ⋆ ⋆ ⋆ ⋆ ⋆ ⋆ ⋆ ⋆ ⋆ ⋆ ⋆ ⋆ ⋆ ⋆

These questions require two skills: (i) an understanding of block graphs, and (ii) the ability to compare the results of one block graph with another. Most children will have encountered block graphs, or histograms, during their mathematics lessons. They need to understand that the quantity of each item or measurement is indicated by the height of the column and that each column represents a different item. In the graphs above, each square represents one goal and each column stands for one football match. One graph indicates the number of goals scored by Heaton United and the other shows how many goals were scored against them.

Question 81 asks for the number of drawn matches. To answer this the child needs to compare the graphs. For example in match 1 (M1), Heaton United scored one goal and had one goal scored against them. Match 2 (M2) was a win for Heaton United because they scored two goals and the opposition scored one goal. In M3 neither side scored a goal and in M4 both teams scored one goal. If the child moves along the columns and counts the number of matches where the same number of goals were scored by both sides, it will be found that there are five such games.